Hull in a Basket

Marcy Jellison

Dedication

In memory of my parents, Pearl and David Freedman, who purchased the property at 7X St. in Hull, in 1954.

Marcy Jellison

Thank you to contributors:

Jim and Marilyn Cleland
Theda and Len Detlor
Anna Levine
Debby Max
Joel Reisman
Yvonne Roen
Arthur Thibeault

Ric Oquita - editing
Victoria Boomsma - color editing
Rebecca Rabinowitz - book design

WAVE Publishing
Hull, MA 2005

ISBN: 0-9785283-0-1
© 2006, Marcy Jellison

Hull in a Basket
Taking the Limerick Challenge

What to do in Hull on a rainy weekend in June, with a house full of guests from out of town? Gathered in the dining room and kitchen, finishing breakfast, Len announces that he's thought of a limerick: *There was a young man from Hull, who found life in the town rather dull. He came by the notion to live on the ocean, and lived out his life as a gull.* That was it. Lots of laughter and the wheels started turning. Standing by the sink over the breakfast dishes, I thought of an opener: *There was a young girl from Nantasket, whose life went to Hull in a Basket...* with five of us around the dining room table, we came up with the rest of it. More laughter. Maybe we should write these down. So I grabbed a large piece of paper, which happened to be the backside of a Chinese takeout menu, and scribbled these little poems down. Debby grabbed the pen and created a "drawing to go with." Thus began the limerick challenge of the summer of 2003.

For the rest of the summer, I had the pleasure of watching my friends and family wander around the house with twisted up expressions on their faces, wracking their brains to come up with rhymes. Try it. It's not so easy.

Hull in a Basket

The following, unless otherwise noted, are written and drawn by me. I've stretched the form a bit. Forgive me. In some cases, I've experimented with internal rhymes. Before long, everything around me became some kind of a limerick. So before going off the deep end, I thought I would put them in a final form and share them with you. It's my valentine to this happy place on earth.

Marcy Jellison
Poet and illustrator

Hull is a Narrow Peninsula

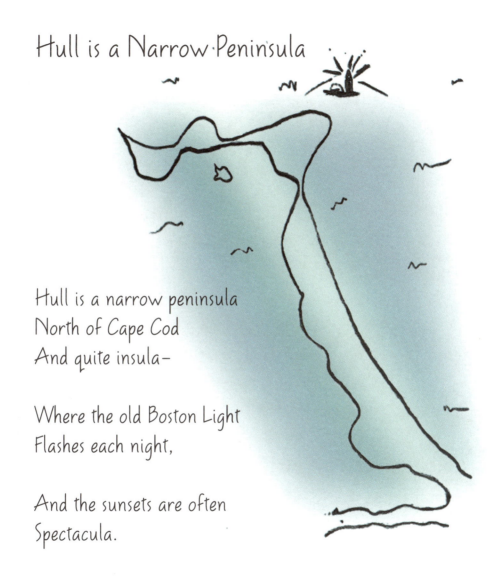

Hull is a narrow peninsula
North of Cape Cod
And quite insula–

Where the old Boston Light
Flashes each night,

And the sunsets are often
Spectacula.

Girl from Nantasket
by Marcy, Theda Detlor, Debby Max, Joel Reisman

There once was a girl from Nantasket
    Whose life went to Hull in a basket.
She was "et" by a fish
    And became a main dish…

And the casserole bowl was her casket.

Young Man from Hull

There was a young man from Hull
Who found life in the town rather dull.

    He came by the notion
        To live on the ocean...

    And lived out his life as a gull.

by Len Detlor

Bluefish
by Yvonne Roen

There was a bluefish from Nantasket
Who suffered from odor quite drastic!

To chase it away,
He swam from the bay…

And plucked some beach roses to mask it.

The Water in Hull is So Cold

The water in Hull is so cold
    To swim you've got to be bold!

When you go for a dip,
    Dive in past your hip...

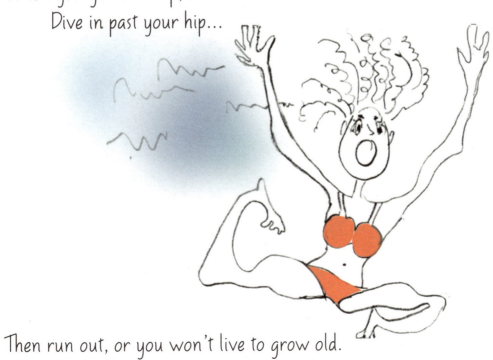

Then run out, or you won't live to grow old.

Lobster

A lobster is a tasty crustacean;
Eating it tests patience and frustration.

To boil it and pull it apart
    You must harden your heart,

But the meat is a rewarding mastication.

Hermit Crab

In Nantasket a small hermit crab
Thought the tide pools at Allerton fab.

He found a periwinkle shell
And said, "What the hell,"

And moved in without paying the tab.

Lady from Hull

There once was a lady from Hull
Who was one day attacked by a gull.

They heard her loud shriek
And searched for a week,

But all that they found was her skull.

Dog

by Arthur Thibeault

There once was a dog from Nantasket

Who always played fetch
If you asked it .

He said with a bark
As it grew dark,

"Please bring me a bone in a basket."

Snake

The children love seeing the snake
Who coils in the hollyhocks' wake.

    They tiptoe and stare
     To see if she's there

Asleep in the sun, on her break.

Garden at 7 X Street

Sitting among my flowers
Pen in hand for hours

Watching a bee
      Listening to the sea. . .

Loosing my mental powers.

Grasshopper

"Mr. Grasshopper, I beg your pardon…
Climbing the screen door is 'forbarden.'"

His little black knees
Propelled his body with ease

And he tragected back into the garden.

Point Allerton

In July, you'll find Queen Ann's lace;
In December, the wind whips your face.

But the rocks abound
On this beach all year round,

And the fishermen just love this place.

Storm

Thunder and sky splitting lightning
On the ocean is thrillingly frightening.

Words can't explain,
    The smell of sea mixed with rain

Or why the horizon appears to be brightening.

Nature

Rolling waves and the sound of the surf
Calm the mind and give spiritual mirth.

Sometimes seaweed and flies
Are the season's demise…

But that's nature, it goes with the turf.

A Little History

Hull's hero, Captain Joshua James
Braved storms to save folks of many names.

His niece, soprano Bernice Di Pasquale,
At the Met sang many a grand opera finale.

Did you know Hull could boast of such claims?

Nantasket Beach

Approaching the beach at low tide
The expanse of sand, so wide

Tiny sandpipers pass
        While you look for sea glass

And the boys on their boards deftly glide...

Ricardo

There once was a tall Argentine
Who became a dear friend of mine.

He graced my house by the sea;
Painted, weeded, cooked
    and played piano for me...

How could I not think him divine?

Sunrise

My kayak on the beach
    at sunrise–
Where a broad path of gold
    greets my eyes

Putting in past the waves,
    On the path the sun paves–

At one with the sea and the skies.

Rocks

When Hullonians go for beach walks,
    They can't resist searching for rocks—

Colors, shapes and striations;
    Variations tickle imaginations

Home collections can grow like a pox.

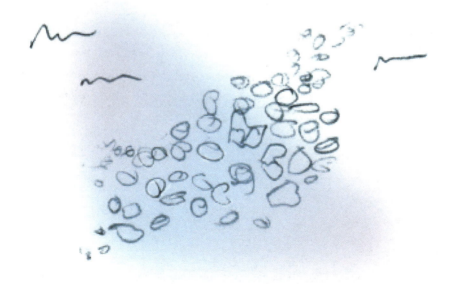

Family

Four boys and a girl, ages 9 and under
With love, my heart's torn asunder.

Their weeks at the beach,
      Simple treasured moments each—

Through their eyes, life's meaning and wonder.

Neighbors

Ubiquitous conversations with neighbors
'Bout houses and garden labors—

The consumption of wine
      Is simply divine,

The food off the grill full of flavors.

September Sunset

In the kitchen, alone, making dinner
    A glow hints of a promising beginner.

Walk down the street, through the lot
    To the bay, where you've got –

An overhead view that's a winner.

Mussel Feast

On the bay, when you hear a ker-plop,
It's a seagull who's making a drop.

He's preparing to eat
Some sweet mussel meat—

For it's easier to smash than to chop.

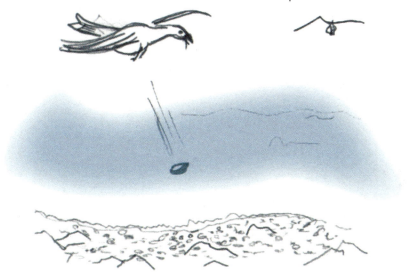

Brunch on the Front Porch

Ron, Jen, Bill, Holly and Megan
Bernie, Butch, Marilyn, Marcy—
    none of us vegan

Breakfasting on tons
Of Ron's delicious cinnamon buns...

Eggs, ham, oatmeal, bread pudding
Coffee and melon — What, no bacon?

Today on Our Way

by Jim and Marilyn Cleland

Today on our way down to Hull,
We remembered our limericks are dull

So we took a quick right
    With intent to take flight

Will our friendship with Marcy be null?

Lady From a Street Named X

by Len Detlor

The lady from a street named X
Quite attractive to the opposite sex

   Her mellifluous voice,
      Was an item of choice,

And her presence it never would vex.

A Toast

To our beach house at 7X
The inspiration for all of this text,

Four generations under your roof
Whose memories are proof...

We shall preserve you and pass you on to the next!

Wave Publishing

Wave Publishing is a part of Hull High School where students learn the craft and business of publishing.

This book was produced by the following members of the freshmen, sophomore, junior, and senior classes under the direction of instructor, Kelly Shanahan and Kathy Andrade, Project Manager.

Kelly Shanahan, Instructor
Kathy Andrade, '07 Project Manager
Steve Costa- '05
Nevin Fitzgerald- '05
Mike Lyons- '05
Jeannine Mooney- '06
Lisa O'rourke- '06
Sean Berard- '07
TJ Bright- '07
Andrew Gorman- '07
Doug Harrington- '07
Bonnie Murphy- '07
Kayla Dennett– '08
Cassy Douglass- '08

Marcy's beloved three bed room beach house (ca. 1889) is available for short term rental all year long and is hauntingly beautiful in the winter as well as loads of fun in the summer.

To order copies of **Hull in a Basket** or to find out about renting the house, visit **www.marcyjellison.com**